SHEARSMAN

141 & 142

WINTER 2024 / 2025

GUEST EDITOR
KELVIN CORCORAN

FOUNDING EDITOR
TONY FRAZER

Shearsman magazine is published in the United Kingdom by
Shearsman Books Ltd
P.O. Box 4239
Swindon
SN3 9FL

Registered office: 30–31 St James Place, Mangotsfield, Bristol BS16 9JB
(this address not for correspondence)

www.shearsman.com

ISBN 978-1-84861-934-0
ISSN 0260-8049

Subscriptions and single copies

Current subscriptions – covering two double-issues, each around 100 pages in length – cost £17 for delivery to UK addresses, £24 for the rest of Europe (including the Republic of Ireland), £28 for Asia & North America, and £30 for Australia, New Zealand and Singapore. Longer subscriptions may be had for a pro-rata higher payment. Purchasers in North America and Australia will find that buying single copies from online retailers there will be cheaper than subscribing, especially following recent drastic price-rises for international mail. This is because copies are printed locally to meet such orders from online retailers. Due to the changes in 2021 regarding the treatment of low-value cross-border transactions in the EU, purchasers in the EU (except for those in Ireland) are recommended to use EU-based online retailers, although these can sometimes be a little slow to update their databases for non-domestic publications.

Back issues from n⁰ 63 onwards (uniform with this issue) cost £9.95 / $17 through retail outlets. Single copies can be ordered for £9.95 direct from the press, post-free within the UK, through the Shearsman Books online store, or from bookshops. Contact us regarding earlier issues (i.e. nos. 1–62), whether for single copies or a complete run.

Submissions

Shearsman operates a submissions-window system, whereby submissions may only be made during the months of March and September, when selections are made for the October and April issues, respectively. Submissions may be sent by mail or email, but email attachments are only accepted in PDF form; submissions may also be made through the upload portal on the Shearsman website (on the *Contact* page). We aim to respond within 3 months of the window's closure, although we do sometimes take a little longer.

This issue has been set in Arno Pro, with titling in Argumentum. The flyleaf is set in Trend Sans.

Contents

Paula Sankelo

Isfjorden

Dream of a fulmar's cry, expect the first snow on the plateau.
Hitch up the half-loaded rifle, cross no path

and if you must encounter a hope
resolve to render it nameless.

Expect, at last, to see the glow of the sea ice
beyond the horizon

and a fulmar feather
fall, shuddering, under the darkening cloud.

§

We lived through the hottest summer, meltwater
wiped out all of the bridge and half my sleep

how the neighbours filled out! Barrel-shaped
they forage the button-like mushrooms

at the back of the house. When I pass them close
they side-step hardly enough to wobble

bloody ribbons peeling from their crowns of bone
they kneel to the migrant sun.

§

A pod of belugas shrill in the fjord
a cod takes the hook through the eye

my child pulls the body over gunwale
determined and shaken

he doesn't hear our praise, or how
the blind one voicelessly cries for her innards

tossed on the waves for the bickering gulls
how a walrus snorts: be on your way!

Later we find the hearing aid in the cold shed
sounding alone in the dark.

§

Kitchen smells of death

my bare hands tear the skin and the chalk-white
plumage from the ptarmigan flesh, and find
in the heart's slick chamber
a single drop of lead

don't think: like a secret

that ended the flight.
          The after-shot silence

is not reflected by the ice
does not ring on the snow.

§

The frames are erected facing the glacier:

mother and child, strung up with care
missing their gentle hooves.

Dusk gives the flesh side
a bluish shimmer

katabatic wind ripples the fur side
into a pattern

never seen on the living.

§

Your antler fell
like a giant eye-tooth lost

or an ossified rhythm silenced
at the edge of comprehension.

How will you sleep now? Will the remaining antler
twist your head, as it nods in slumber
give you a crick in the neck?

I held my breath   you dropped it.

There's a hole in the world and the light runs out.

I wonder how we'll settle down for the night
and how could you shed your antler   here comes the snow.

Huw Gwynn-Jones

Four Welsh Words for Water

Chwys:
/χwɨːs/

German 'Schweiss', Sanskrit 'svedas'

Perspiration, sweat, beads of moisture
oozing like a cheese. Diaphoresis.

A state of worry, anxiety or distress
moil and hustle.

'Chwys y fwyall' – a folk remedy
for ringworm, the sweat or condensation
formed on the blade of an axe
held over burning hay.

'Chwys Arthur' – meadowsweet

Niwl, Nifwl:
/nɪʊl/

Gaelic 'neul', Icelandic 'nifl'
Nordic 'nibelheim' – misty home
of the ice kingdom, one of the Nine
Realms where Nibelung dwell.

Fog, mist, vapour, haze – that which
obscures and confuses, isolates.

A place of loss, the dampness
of dead men's breath.

'Fel hwrdd mewn niwl' – a helpless state
('like a ram in the fog')

Glaw, gwlaw   Breton 'glav', Sanskrit 'jalá'
/gla.u/   Proto-Indo-European 'jalám'

Drizzle, deluge, rain and smirr. That
which falls and cleanses. Memory
of life inside the nimbus, freeze and
fall and all things hydrological.

Lacrimosa. The sadness of tears.

'Glaw Mai' – first May rain, reputed
to be good for weak eyes and for
killing lice in cattle.

Môr   Proto-Celtic 'mori', French 'la mer'
/moːr/   Old Church Slavonic 'morje'

Ocean, briny, sea, the drink.

Gaudí's cathedral of light
between the waves. A notion
of haven, polestar and petrel. Worlds
without walls, caressed by a movement
of blue or darker hue.

Place of Dutchmen, phantom
sails and old men obsessed
by whales and tales of Scylla

swirl and maelstrom. The whip
and heave of a ship, the gathering
of souls, the reek of fish.

'Gwas y weilgi' – 'son of the sea' or 'sea-wolf'
                    – Albatross

A Feeling for Stone

Fall   Come summer, come nights of long-
         tailed stones and comets, come every
         "Lucy in the Sky" who rides the flux

         of suns – the "bright white", Celan's
         bringers of light whose fall is fire
         and coldstone, cairn and clogfaen

Abrasion   You might start with a story
         a tale of odyssey, let it take you

         where it will, this dream you have
         of a crossing, of barren lands

         and rapids, the thud of stones, journey
         to the heart of a dark wood

         at night, the words you let slip
         and those you leave in the trees

         where they etch their acidity
         their scouring of innocent things

Marble   Or you could look into the rock from which
         you are hewn, as did Isaiah, where you might
         feel the broad stretch of a quarryman's back
         or the heft in a stonemason's arms, meet the eyes
         of fine Renaissance man sculpting stone
         into elegance, softness and skin, as he listens
         to the clef of the marble's song, tastes its acrid
         tears, intimations of a dusty mortality

Slate   Something quite satisfying
about the quiescence of slate

something pleasing
about folios of metamorphic
rock cut clean

something quite fine
in the indifference of clay
and dull quartz worn smooth

Chambered Cairn
where the light is flat

unhurried
made to last

no trace of breath
nor undertone

just stasis
and settled stone

its lichenous
cast of green

inscrutable
serene

And Rise Celan again, "As one speaks
to stone, as / you, / to me
from the abyss"

or Rilke, "One moment
your life is a stone in you,
and the next, a star"

What It Is to Rise

We were always mountain folk
from the day she bore us
                carved us
from obsidian and clay

she
who loomed
        aloof and enigmatic
                the heft
and sway of her

who watched us run wild beneath
her icy peaks
        become nimble
                immune to cold

and taught us all there was to know
about height
        verticality
                and what it meant
to rise like a thermal
        like a condor in flight.

~~

You should have seen her dress
those days of spring
        the way she stepped out
full of song
        all hillsweet
                and earth-high

and though we thought
we knew her moods
                    her dark and
windwhite ways

in truth
she served only the light
                    knew only
how to pierce a pane of sky
in search of cirrus
                and contrails
                        and noctilucent blue.

Carmen Bugan

Hawk

I went out to look at him –
An apparition with great wings
Glowing in the light of morning,
Scanning below the spring tree line.
I returned inside and drank my tea
Without losing sight of him.
The orioles put on alarm calls,
Mockingbirds attacked him,
He now cleans his feathers, unperturbed,
At the very top of the tallest tree.

I think about my deadlines
And the morning sliding by,
But he watches my garden
From way up there.
I am hooked on him
Against the flawless sky
With nearly flowering trees below,
Time pulling the two of us along,
In the bright, fresh morning.

Under him, such a tiny tree branch
Sustains unbearable weight,
Fragility seems only an illusion.
Hawk, take everything that is weak in me
In your claws: eat it.
Leave me wise and patient.
It's been nearly two hours since
You appeared, and straightened me
From the spine up, eyes on you.

Solar eclipse

Snowy egrets flew just above our heads,
Waded at the water's edge.

A blue-grey heron
Roosted in the yellow magnolia.

Cormorants flapped their wings
On the floating tree trunks in the pond.

Geese talked in pairs.
Swans napped over their nests.

A row of turtles sunned themselves.
The moon slid over the sun like an eyelid

And everything went cool and quiet.
My kids whispered of sunset,

The spring flowers glowed in the field.
And then the moon slid off the sun

Returning all the songs to the birds.
We are changed forever, having witnessed

Night inside the day, having
Heard the wings of snowy egrets.

Josephine Balmer

Victim Statement

(Persian empire, 480 BCE)

Among the many Panionius had mutilated
Hermotimus was perhaps the most exalted…
(Herodotus, 8.105.)

By chance I saw him again, the man
who had wielded the knife. I remember
how he'd hacked as if stemming cancer
or slicing an arrow shaft from a wound
that was already infected, festering.

> *… so much blood*
> *I don't know how I am still alive…*

Recognition was raw, a spreading rash.
Still I greeted him as an old friend,
well-met. I owed him a debt, I said:
I was favoured, at the King's side.
And I could give him his full share
of fortune if he followed me to Sardis
with his wife and sons – my guests.
In the city I would make full redress
for everything he had done for me.

> *… I often think*
> *of suicide…*

Perhaps he believed that the gods
kept their eyes shut. That the odds
were still stacked against justice.
In Sardis I compelled him to castrate

his sons. At blade point I forced
them to neuter their father in return.
He had turned me into nothing. No
one. And here he was, ensnared,
recast, by his own gore-soaked trap.
I was someone. I felt something.
Disgust. Desolation. Despair

> *... if there's a hell somewhere*
> *it's worse than that...*

(Italic quotes based on: 'She Thought She Was Unshockable
Then Two Castrated Ukrainian Soldiers Arrived',
Christina Lamb, *The Sunday Times*, 18/06/2023)

Burying the Bones
(Teutoburg Forest, Germany, 15 CE)

> *Marching at the furthest frontier of empire,*
> *the legions came to the site of the massacre...*
> (Tacitus, Annals, 1.60)

We saw the flash of white first, scattered
over fields or heaped like shovelled snow.
We walked on slaughter. Shards shattered –
skull scraps, spine slivers – beneath the groves

as the light congealed. Decomposed heads,
hacked from the corpses of fellow soldiers,
hung like roosting bats or a rotting harvest,
their mouths drooping in a howl of horror.

By now we could not tell which was joined
with which. But we collected up those parts
like family, like strangers, lovers mourned
too soon; blood of our blood, buried at last.

In grief and rage we wept as if for old friends
at the confusion of war, the cost. At how it ends.

Iapyx's Gift

My brother Icarus fell from searing
skies. I fell in love with their god.

Apollo's passion was overpowering,
jagged, scalding. Soon he offered me
his scorched skills: poetry, prophecy.

But I had held him as he'd shuddered
into sweating visions, tasted his sooted
kisses, his lips charred by ashen dread.

So I chose healing. I knew he'd leave.
But my father Daedalus, fresh-bereaved,
bewildered, was lost in his own labyrinths

on fractured paths. What use prescience
as the past slowly slipped from his grasp?
I bartered hope with my lover god. I asked

for the cures, the herbs and hidden remedies
that might repair minds as well as bodies.
This was my gift to the future. Yet still

I missed him, his skin on mine, lightning
on a summer's day, his breath like flame;
the graze of his fingers, arrows sharpened.

On blistered nights my father calls my name.
Apollo, my lover, has forgotten who I am.

Carrie Etter

The Selves

a ten-year-old girl who writes a play
and commands her friends to their parts

an editorial assistant
who collects enough couch change
to buy hot and sour soup for dinner

an angel of grief

a nineteen-year-old crossing L.A. by bus
as a man draws a finger up her leg

a seventeen-year-old
who smooths her extended belly in circles,
whispers a lullaby

a boy climbing a pine tree

a three-year-old who reads or
pretends to read *How Puppies Are Born*

an undergrad who shows up for her Latin final with
Kleenex, lozenges, juice, and coffee

a twenty-six-year-old rollerblading, soaring
alongside the Pacific
from Venice to Redondo Beach

a young man strutting

an American at The Star in Bath
asked to explain Trump

a tapir nosing into shade

the only girl of 15 staff
on a campground maintenance crew

a Midwestern tuna casserole spiked with cayenne

a teen employee who, in an empty
Arby's Roast Beef, sings
to the radio's "American Pie"

a woman lying on her back in the grass
during a meteor shower

a clitoris blooming under a tongue

a woman confronting her father's
pulmonologist, cardiologist: "How many months?"

a teenager, on the wrong floor of the university library,
chancing on the lit mags

an angel of summer, or of loss, or of a
motel room during the apocalypse

a minor poet who teems nonetheless

a milkweed pod releasing its seeds to the wind

Project Cannikin

Amchitka Island, Alaska, 6 November 1971

Up goes the island! Up, up, up! We're testing a nuclear missile!

Up goes the island! And a man brought his wife and daughters to see it.

Up goes the island–twenty-five feet! Down come a thousand dead sea otters.

Down comes the island, down come cliffs, rocks, cormorants, eagles, falcons, ducks…

(crushed skulls) (ruptured lungs) (snapped spines)

Nine-year-old Emily said, "It was kind of like a train ride."

Jim Jones's Last Sermon

'Excerpts From Transcript of Tape Describing Final Moments at Jonestown,' *The New York Times*, 15 March 1978

We've been so betrayed. We have been so terribly betrayed. / …be kind to children, and be kind to seniors, and take the potion like they used to do in ancient Greece, and step over quietly…. / I'm the best thing you'll ever have. / I'm gonna lay down my burden. Down by the riverside. / Please, please, please, please, please, please, please. / Say peace. Say peace. / Can we hasten with our medication? / Rise in the morning and not knowing what's going to be the night's bringing. / [Children crying.] / Children, it will not hurt. / [Children crying.] / Hurry. Hurry, my children. Hurry.

The Lawn

O Middle America, does it all come down to a perfectly trimmed lawn? One evenly sprayed against dandelion and shepherd's purse, toward a uniformity of shape and color. Some summers, the Etters proved the embarrassment of Arlington Drive, grass a half-foot high, dandelions rife, children–theirs and others–shouting, cartwheeling, running, clapping. You could tell, just looking at that lawn, that at least one of those Etter girls would get pregnant out of marriage, and what about the one who spent eighteen months in jail? The house's new owners, now they keep the lawn tidy. There's no story to tell about them.

Night England by Train

Swathes of black where I imagine fields, sheep.
If there's light, there's concrete.

On a platform's edge, leafless bushes scratch the air.
A pair of eyes, glimpse of orange fur.

Swish of tail.
The train begins again, charges west

toward a cold, black sea.
Come, it calls, but not to sleep.

Ian Seed

For Keeps

Lone, nocturnal towards the end
when we need reassurance
or twilight to give a glimpse
not a delusion or a ghost
sitting with sleeves rolled up
on a rustic bench, I want

yet not quite want the pretty
girl shaking her salad dry
with a bit of madness at the edge
of the canal, thinking of the vision
that still tows, my intestines
freezing, my face muddy, I sit here

rather than smear and blur and fail
in a dead-end hotel. The sky itself
is terribly uncertain. There is no room
for reality between the two bridges.
What I have seen on the road
remains in my head, trapped

in one perspective, the filthiness
of an isolated house, even though
here and there, we laugh, trying
to recall when we got off work
and were once free and easy.
I come to a waterfall by conjoining

the chapters of the swollen stream.
Come back, now and again, my boys
even with your fatal sinfulness. This too
is unconvincing. It was again a fine day.

We have netted it. Some good sailors
are here to gather shells. The tides

have their prestige. They are lovely
and impenitent. If we look at our reflections –
we are a pair! Let's make a point
of following each other down to the pools,
under the scrutiny of the gentlemen in blue
who now approach to soften the whole business.

Seemingly

The distraction of that one, but not now,
not yet, even if we're mostly up for it
at this time of night before the moisture
of dawn. I wouldn't fancy being out

dragged along the cobbles. There's the hill
we sometimes stand on to watch the old
house and the town beyond. There used to be
another coughing in the alleyway

from an upside-down belly, face up
to God, who's here, but the lambs in the fields
behind us have it all. It's no boner
to admit it ruins the mood. That's quite

an interruption when the big sky lid
slams down, and yet it is everything
to us, coming over the hill not
for the first time not knowing the worst.

Trick-kissed

You push through, finding yourself behind the curtains,
the earliest of the party, in what turns out to be a walk of shame.
Consider yourself a stranger in this country. Wait until the end
of the act of secret gratification, at the appointed hour

with the very same man you say you love, a man silhouetted,
with the worst of faces, continually passing in the street
but you don't love him enough. Nerves surge, to be sure.
He comes closer to ease the business. Why not?

The girl at the bar was found to be dislocated, still
so obedient. She has an amazing body actually, already
burning the stranger and with the pressing, if passionless,
invitation of the curve of her breasts, he has entangled himself

so far as to undress her soft, fine fabric in the cheerfullest
manner, if without deftness. And what are you doing?
Frying peaches in butter! C'est drôle, c'est vrai. She's wet
with a jolt, and her tears when they fall are swift and bright

Simon Smith / Du Fu

Reflections on Li Bai This Winter's Day
(*for Anthony Mellors*)

in the lonely quiet of my study

I circle back reflecting on you solely through the early hours

yet again I reach down the tale of the magnificent tree

fish out & recite the ode of the 'Horn-bow'

wet & cold seep through my threadbare shirt transparent

you're wandering about I know it in search of the magic

& I'd be away in a flash to walk by your side

we dreamt together & thought together through our solitudes

Book 1 Poem 27

Quarantined in Spring

the country torn apart rivers & mountains always just *there*

it's springtime in the city the trees & grasses greening

wrenched apart with the separation the flowers weep as I do

alert to Time slipping away the heart awake to the birds

the fires of war burn wear down a third month

for a single word from home I'd pay out infinite ransom

white hair thinning pulled away & out strand by strand

not enough left to be twisted upwards by a hair-clasp

Book 4 Poem 25

Thought Notes by Night Travel

beside the estuary's shoreline thin grasses spun with thinnest winds

the mast disappears far into the dark above my boat

suspended the stars gaze over the wide & endless flatlands

the moon's intensity reflected back into the Great River's wave

the pursuit of Literature will find no name for me

aged & ill I ought to resign from my job

sailing sailing all aims to the winds who am I

across the sky to the land a seagull cart-wheels alone

Book 14 Poem 63

On Studying Fireflies

on this evening of an Indian summer fireflies drift in off the Magic Mountain

around blinds tipped half-opened half-closed by design stick to my coat glowing

started from a dream sat up in my den lyre & books stone cold

out there from under the roof their light pulses to mingle with galaxies fading

they waft up & over the drinking well multiplying their number light on light

moment by moment they invent the luminous flower petals blossoms passing

      here then gone

beside the grey river an ocean my hair fades into whiteness you into sadness

next year when it will be as it will & me home or exiled

Book 19 Poem 28

A Seasoned Wanderer

my journeying has taught me how to treat loved ones

throughout my long life I have experienced many simple feelings

looking older for a moment I can laugh at myself

some *petits fonctionnaires* have picked on me with casual malice

departing the country's metropolis left Wang Can inconsolable

a dull ennui drove Jia Yi to a nervous breakdown

& yet the city foxes don't write the history books

it's the roaming tigers & hyenas that steal the show

Book 22 Poem 20

Sujatha Menon

The Surface Area of a Nightmare

Horse burial = $\dfrac{\text{L x W}}{\text{moon}}$: rectangle

Cilia swept   lying labial in a tangled mane was no place for a
          sleeping woman,
though I liked the weave   and how it prevented cysts easily formed
around a crease or a partially dissolved hoof. How was I to know
that this was not the length of heaven or the width
of a bogus hell constricting.   There was a crescent sky but no half-moon.
Such was the order of shapes.

Broken window = $A^2 - ? \times 100$: square

I've bled on its edge many times before   looking for
answers flicking up like shards of crystalised piss   rising up
like the machines, overwhelmed and overheating.   They pose
as lumens though neither open ended or closed, circular, squared or
          arched;
shatter like children whose mothers did not come from mothers but
          from mares
and areas$^2 - ? \times 100$. This is how the darkness gets in and unpacks itself.

Witches hat = $1/2 \, b \times h +$ what's underneath : triangle

The place where the hypotemuse rattles though we still don't know at
          what angle
she spins or the length of her very dark side dividing
like a guarded spell passed down in degrees.   They call her the 'difficult one'
impenetrable, obtuse and uneven even in tone   those shades of blackness
unclassified. This apparently, provides inspiration if not a common point
to ponder the horror   also known as a sharpened vertex (or tooth).

Platelets = πr^2 x heat (this is also a vent diagram)™ : circle

This is how the night clots around the moon
marrow- osteoporotic yet milky in its venomous return to
curdle sleep like a vascular churning of black butter.
There is no mistaking the similarity to a soothless lullaby –
ineffective   infecting   injecting
half dreams with liquid song, quavers sticking together:

R oc   kab yeba   by

ont he t   reet   o   p

h   o   tt   e r

Snout of a shovel = ½ (a + b) – free speech : trapezoid

A septal deviation <<< subcranial speech and truffles
rare like pignut gold. When you arrived digging for tails
of the alphabet, trying to colonise
thoughts not yet formed, I built a castle around
the letters 't' & 'b' should they sprout and escape down the
shanks of throats. When speech is never straight or forwards
but bent to the shape of the night pulled downwards –
imagination is mute.

Timed egg = πab{ ‰ } : ellipse

Stuffed into an hourglass pie with a penny stuck in the narrowing
splitting head and tail
is an eggless chicken whose time ran out
into the road, belly spawning
like a ripened appendix far away from A & E.
This can be added to the list of things like cheese and whale-grain caviar
that must not be eaten before bed. There is danger of incubation
in the scrambled night.

Note: The folds of the endoplasmic reticulum's membrane are called cisternae. These flattened membrane sacs give the organelle more space to create proteins and other important molecules. The singular form, cisterna also refers to a reservoir or tank for holding water, especially a tank for storing rainwater. In anatomy it is used to describe a space that is filled with body fluid.

The First Farmers were Sheet Breeders

The seed cleaners gathered in their luminous fold, began to polish
bare words beneath breath. Only now do we know they were harvesting
eggs with no instructions other than to sieve very gently
should the lumen appear and then disappear.

Every kernel, pip, ovule and stone shook
to its ectoplasmic cocoon,
complained of names that would never fruit gold
or bear resemblance to the truth – fat and phasmaphobic.

With no need for sleep, water or food
they tapered into strange yellow hues,
longed for the call of their wild and ancestral roots

and then blushed, no longer revealing invisible.

Note: Through the process of domesticating wild carrots over thousands of years, they turned from a ghostly white to Dayglo orange.

Transcendental Eradication

via sorbitol traps and spice trade maps
they arrived in a Firebird Spittle,
moaned about the wind and the turn
in the weather with their
fangs dissolving and roots hanging out.
In the cavernous pit stop of the mouth
the molar bears huddled-
the lick of extinction
would soon take them out
and all who witnessed crumbled,
collapsed into knots then escaped
on a cough-
that felt like levitation.
***

In a new life in the old world
where drones were clumping,
we sang songs about peace
and how fish were falling
out of the sky.

Mycobacterium tuberculosis (Mtb) is a bacterial pathogen that causes Tuberculosis (TB), a devastating disease that is the leading infectious cause of death in the world. Mtb has developed cunning tactics to survive in the human body for decades. Research has discovered that it feeds on certain sugars thus possessing a deadly 'sweet tooth'. Scientists are currently working on how to starve it.

Mischa Foster Poole

stick losers

they have been popping as you said all night stick
losers   gauche erasure poems   transluce
I hate your cup of milk and Arthur sits in the cave
its ganaches round the edge   bad taste   you take
one large chunk out of   a cup of tea
what a pile of stuff to move about!   I hate stuff!
a shuffling grain on a belt   displacement of nibs
an archimedes screw   let's go for a burger
and a flute of champagne (sic) the day's clear
I hate daffodils

xxvi

autumn excess
each goldfish recovers
after an accompanying voucher
swamped, spits,
squeezes, mills at a rate
the creator wound,
seeds a rhetorical controller
the thesis bridge
the funnest vessel claims
a convict genre

folded. Another pat
the dusty vein
starved past a dictionary

in origin
how does the bone compact?
an irrational track you've offset
a gay sock rested orbital amplifier:
every compact revival
is also an intelligence

xxxvi

Or if something landed comes, or big
in its proximity, it is quite what you imagined.

But steps off the running board perhaps too lightly,
and you redress the impulse to throw arms

either down, or around its neck.
For it is not the first time you have tapped the wrong

person, or laid arms around what
you thought was a lover.

Perhaps I do mean grounded. But if so,
more in an electrical sense,

and it is with a struggle to fathom
which, or whether, currents running alongside

are streams within which swim compassion,
or light, and wholly justifiable, indifference.

xxxvii

Going against the grain (provided there is
an accommodation of facts supporting
for or against) gradually — this

cannot be said to abandon the light touch
characteristic of a descent by sycamore
or an overripe peach rolling a handspan
counter-clockwise inwards at you.

It is improbable that the immediate world
should simply present itself to you

but if you step back, where a pane was obscured
through a certain precise refraction of light
it now becomes a through-line
towards attaining a non-miserable future derivative.

xxxviii

I say approximate because, unwilling to dash myself
against it I instead roll this large boulder slightly
more towards the wings. In spite of the cost
I do so with the finesse called for by a rehearsed end.

How gradually, you think to yourself, how opportunely
you flex to raise yourself into the remarkable.
Into the remarkable, and this, I would say, is the very least.

Rimas Uzgiris

At the Exhibition

I'm trying to figure out how he did the rain,
the engraved dashes of a sharpened tool
exposing the absence, or the void, behind color,
and my son is pulling at my arm:
he wants me to see the lego wave,
and I'm pulling at my wife's arm:
I want her to see the woman and the octopus,
something like Proteus taking tentacled form,
an old god of the world, wrapping
the fisherman's wife in pleasure, oh,
and my daughter is pulling at my arm:
she wants me to see the horsies of
Hokusai, Hiroshige and others. Who?
Contemporaries. I try to learn their names.
It's hopeless. People. Persons. When
you watch TV or listen to political debates,
it all seems hopeless: no one cares
about art, poetry, but here, it's a crowd:
art lovers, curious citizens, looking,
reading, listening. And where are we,
most of the time, in this culture?
Bombs are falling, fumes are bubbling,
garbage swirls in the oceans
like a mythological island on which
Odysseus would be detained, bound
and gagged by our Circe of plastic:
he's never going to get back home. Sometimes,
I want to retreat to a bamboo grove
like the seven sages of classical China,
write poems on bark, fog for a blanket,
clouds pillowing my head, but who

am I kidding? I fly back and forth
between North America and Europe,
live in a comfortable apartment,
go to the pharmacy for my insulin:
I'm not about to move to the fucking woods.
So I walk through this forest of limbs
with eyes committed to seeing: the startling blues
of cataracts, shy courtesans on straw mats,
pompous actors like peacocks on display,
regular citizens hunched under obsidian rain,
a fisherman poling under the sodden alphabet of a bridge,
motley ducks cavorting on grey washes (and here
I recall W. Homer's duck in midair, a muzzle's
tongue of flame licking the forest), and a relentless wave
made of legos, reiterated in recycled bottles, in multiple
applications of ink, washing over us, engulfing us:
there is nowhere to go. We are really in it.

Talking to My Daughter

The catbird jugs in the backyard bush.
Scratch that. It screeches and whistles.
What's that? says my daughter. A catbird.
Does it look like a cat? No, it sounds
like one though. Listen _____ . Oh.
Meow. Night falls. There's the Big Dipper.
What's that? Stars, shaped like a ladle.
See? OK. It's part of Ursa Major. What-a
what? The Great Bear. I don't see a bear.
Neither do I. Never did. But there's
the North Star. Follow the ends of the ladle.
OK. Is that where Jesus was born? Yes,
well, sort of. Maybe not. Bethlehem.
But the Three Kings followed the star,
though maybe that was a different star,

I'm not sure anymore. Did they bring gifts?
Yes. A Teddy Bear? No. Gold, incense.
What's that? Smelly stuff. Oh. Time for bed.
Let's read Paddington. Ursa Minor.
What? Nothing. Corduroy, Pooh.
Daddy, why do we like bears so much?
I don't know, they're not so cute in real life.
Have you met one? Yes. Were you scared?
Yes. But these are friendly bears. OK.
Good night. Good night. Sweet dreams.
Sweet – you know how you shuffle off to bed
sometimes, wondering what it is you're
doing here, and the universe is so vast,
and it's like you knew something but forgot,
and you're just hoping you can love someone
in the right way, for as long as it takes,
but what's the right way, and takes to what? –
Dreams of plush bears dancing to the catbird's
improvisatory, ragtime jug. That'll do, for now.

Freunde

was the name of the restaurant,
and no, they didn't play Beethoven,
though they did host our Versopolis dinner party
in which we were friends, or at least friendly,
and recited odes to joy, or melancholy,
as happens to the best of us.
It was all served up with wine and cheese,
which may have come later, after
Patrick turned to me and said,
"This one's too abstract." Yes, I thought,
its angels could use a bit of grit,
more reality, so to speak, talking trash,
whispering weird words. Maybe

our thoughts are generally too grand
and banal at the same time
like a sudden summer storm
along the Keizersgracht
which tears a single leaf from a linden tree.
(Please don't call them lime trees. No limes
will be sliced in the making of this poem,
though maybe a finger, and soon.)
Is that too abstract?
Is there enough grit in the teeth of my abstraction?
I think we need some philosophical advice.
Ouch! A paper cut.
Plato's Complete Works, tr. Jowett,
where it says we first learn from bodies
about Beauty, which sounds fun,
if you can get it, and I did
meet many nice people from all over Europe
("if there were sex in friendship…")
but not the one I most wanted to meet:
She was Beauty Itself. Cutting
me down
to size. Or
is that time? Plato
would disagree
but he's too abstract — which
has the advantage of being like a leaf
not stripped by storm, a finger
not smarting, though,
at this point, it's just a memory.
Like a first friend. The form of
another life. A better one.
The right forms, he tells us, never die.

Jazmine Linklater

Free Time Song

Dusk again when the parakeets fly
overhead to wherever they're heading.
Next time will be dawn, you'll be
sleeping or drinking your coffee
and waiting for energy
and light to emerge
from the silvery night
you're just entering.
It is 6:41. The violet
air sparks a process
you don't understand,
enables the decorations
you'd hopefully hung
on the walls of the yard
to burst into being,
emitting the energy
they've absorbed from
the sun you've not sat in
all day. Your light is blue,
so you think of the poets of blue
as dusk rests against red brick,
tinting a purplish bruise on the day
you have wasted productively, wilfully
urging the hours to pass as the parakeets pass overhead
twice a day, whether you're watching or waiting or not.
A pattern's emerging that you don't want
to recognise, a colourless seeping out of
the objects you've spread all around you
to mimic a border of safety, a place
where digression is limited
to overhead flights

you observe
from a distance
that stretches
from here
to here only.
As your vision
is shifted
from one vanishing
point to another
on the upsurge of wind
made by the beating of wings
in the setting you're trying to finish
and hold still, you disturb nothing. The table
again, the chair you sink into, drinking a liquid as thin
as events half-remembered from time that was maybe
before, the way dawn was before and again, you emerge
into the twilight tinged green by the parakeets' twice-daily flight
overhead to wherever they're heading.

Blueprint Part-Received

I walked around the city
slowly, drunkenly, on two hours' sleep
and three hash browns, one bloody Mary
and a pint of cider. The sunny glinting
under my umbrella. One foot
following the other and our conversations
bouncing off the hoardings round the monumental
brick facades left over from this city's former revolution
and the glass-front businesses whose purposes
are indiscernible. All my thoughts are overturning
me. It's maybe not romantic
you had said on last night's early morning call
but I want to do this properly. We have to

plan it out to build it right. But is that possible
with walls. We'll move the parts around
to fit the thing we saw on friends'
fridge doors. Laying what out now.
I love you. I put it in this poem
before responsibility forgets
the structure's maintenance
for living in. Where the building
never ends.

The dark grey clouds roll in
between my writing and the sun –
and they will roll
and is that beautiful.
A hoppy sparrow in the puddle – Himalayan balsam
everywhere you look – the bracken. We will be
overcome. But please
don't let me get lost
inside this labyrinth. Is there
sufficiency. I'll look after you
if you'll look after me now. If
I address this poetry to you
will it protect us both from my catastrophising
tendencies. Is that a building block
right there. My head is hurting.
Will you lay your hands over my eyes?
Hold me where you are.
The city's rolling over.
I can feel our structure
drilling down its taproot
laying out its traps.

John Muckle

Fred Karno's Palace

Skiffs clattering down over the rollers, splashed
Into a sea of bright crinoline, boaters, blazers
Flaring in the postcard white-out;
Water-babies breast-stroked fully-clothed
Beside the varnished hulls of pleasure-seekers,
Uniformed servants brewing up onboard,
Rare river flotsam bobbing about at Molesey lock,
Sight-seers milling on the banks for a glimpse
Of so much unfettered womanhood.
It was here they decided to make their homes
Almost by accident, by accident, unplanned.

At night the great Karsino was girdled by
Upended chandeliers, houseboats no longer agitated in the wash
Of barges, steam-powered river craft, fitted dwellings
For sleepy Gods of stage and music hall;
Garrick's domed temple to Shakespear, Fred Karno himself
Not yet tucked up but facing ruin
Due, it was said, to the Gypsies' curse on Tagg's Island:
A wooded teardrop afloat on Father Thames' blood-stream.
Pikeys weren't to blame for Karno's lust for greatness,
Powerless, ridiculous in their filthy rags,
Riding in arrogant pony-carts, their high-rolling poverty
An annoyance still to residents of Hampton and Molesey.
Karno didn't have to sink everything in the Karsino.
Anyway, Thos. Tagg was the original sinner
Who converted the ait from osier-growing beds, booted
The gypsies off to build the first hotel there
& was the first financial basket-case, taking a cold plunge
On the fluctuating fevers of the Edwardian pleasure thermometer.

Two fellows with a big pneumatic hammer
Uninstalled the stone jetty for rowing boats,

Long after Fred was dead & gone, after bankruptcy,
Limped to the coast to buy a half-share in an off-license,
Monies given him by Chaplin, his early protégé.
Somehow our riverine ancestors over-rowed
To clack billiards in its splendid hulk,
An ice-cream sculpted palace, arched Palm Court.
Shut up, landscape-gardened terraces where in 1916
A thousand wounded soldiers were entertained
& officers' wives served limbless men on crutches:
All this impresario's generosity curdled by rot,
Blown over, shrouded & forgotten.
                              Fred Karno's Army:
Epithet for chaos, misdirected energy, rank incompetence.
We are Fred Karno's army, the ragtime infantry,
We cannot shoot, we cannot fight,
What ruddy use are we?
                         Comedy held show-tell-truths
Smuggled across in dumb-show, perfected, unravelled.
Long ago, seems obvious now.
                              Whatever did they speak of
Nobby, Killy, Frank, stretched across still-good baize,
Lining up safety shots on Europe's battlefields?
Tin-pot generals, calm-as, they'd have their own ideas,
Bright somethings, subjects never broached often.
Just things they knew themselves which you couldn't,
Nosey parker, slopey-head stuck in the *Daily Sketch*.
"It's Lobby Ludd," Frank said. "That boy is Lobby
Ludd! You are Lobby Ludd, and I claim my five pounds."
Killy, at the fag-end of Phyllis, out in the garage,
Once-proud speedway ace, designer of "The Yellow Peril";
Nobby, whose son walked a hand-reared fox on a leash…

Eugene Fuller lived opposite my grandmother, wore a beret,
Tinted photographs & painted a portrait of her house,
A Victorian villa for which she miraculously found money.
Eugene had fought in the trenches, sketched in mud & ink
Two men carrying a full stretcher. Lit up by flashbulbs.
A prisoner, he had seen with his own narrowed eyes

Twenty starving men devour a living, breathing cow
Released into their compound by order of a mysterious lady,
A Belgian aristocrat who happened to be passing. She
Didn't *have* to do anything, could just have ridden by.
Old Fuller telling me this, his frail, quivering voice; he
Showed me this technique with postcards, how
He spliced them together, transforming the thus composed
Into a luminous, unified, dappled pictorial surface;
In a draped, dusty dining room his student paintings
Hung like whited sepulchres in heavy guilt frames;
His Belgian wife turned out to be a man named Cecil.

Fred Karno got into films quite late, although
You'd think his invention of short, complex, mimed scenes
& character-based "Sketches" would have made
Him an acknowledged genius director of visual slapstick.
The old goat had made and lost several fortunes already
By the time he came to launch the career of Kitty Kilfoyle
In *Early Birds*, in which Karno played "the Jew".
No particular triumph; you can't help wondering
If she'd kept a weather eye on *Astoria*'s mahogany ceiling.
Probably a welcome change from digs in travelling rep.
However, she was born in Chiswick, not Molesey-o,
She is therefore, as we say, regrettably, not Gloucester,
Therefore no kin of Alice, Allen Aylmer (Killy),
Walt, Kilfoil, Kilfoyl, back to Timothy James of Offaly,
A sergeant in Wellington's army, sometime parked on Malta,
Later a Chelsea butler. Dear lady, making this hopeful error
(Wrongly unacknowledged daughter of Allen Aylmer's boy,
Killed despatch riding while your poor mother held on to you)
Indeed, yes, you are a Kilfoyle & our long lost sister.
Sit at the top of the table, worry about this no longer.
Only the illegitimate. Only the illegitimate are beautiful.
So dutiful in research but leapt to false conclusions.
Oh my poor dear woman, thank you for sharing.

Down an alley to the river. Sweep in on the bright gravel.
Same old stuff the ancestors trod, revised in 1830,

Bare-knuckle fights in the blood-soaked Regency.
A boy born to be a blacksmith, a girl a skivvy.
Is it right, I arks you, is it right? Should husbands work?
Suffragettes razed Hurst Park's racetrack grandstand.
Digitised cylinders click and pop, spring out of their day.
They pulled down Karsino in '72, encrypted video here.
Beside these wide & flowing waters my love & I did plunge
Prone to intentions & unimpeachable fantasies.

I remember the girl Janet in the back garden photo,
En Pointe for the box brownie, perched on a rusty chair
& me beside her, one sandal on a flaking scooter
In long trousers, white shirt, my encephalitic head
Bowed towards her in involuntary sympathy.
I remember her prancing & twirling along beside
High walls of old residences encrusted with wild roses
Down sunny avenues to the Mole. A place such as you
Would like to walk past forever, leading to women
In a lost kitchen, close & clammy with their talk
Georgina Skaif, Lynne Sidaway, Tish & Jennifer Stiles
& that would be probably the last I ever saw of her.

Scurrying lit-up walkways at midnight, electric slippers
& where *does* electricity come from? Doth come from stars?
A return to the past is always a recovery of innocence
Buoyed up by acceleration for a few splashy moves
In the recessed gumshield boating pond of the Upper Deck.
You could watch us paddling in circles from the footpath.
Your mirthless laughter followed us, shading its eyes.

Ellen Harrold

Worker, Queen, Drone.

Were tranquillisers and pretty notions to lie so gently at our feet.
Forsaken expectations built on petty lifetimes
of rules so easily broken.
Gathered in haystacks around the wildflowers,
all bowing to the wind and rain.
Nettles thrive as grass cut to pleasing view
yet even these are gentle things
gifting so graciously
soup, tea.
Should we be so welcome in the homes of others
left despised.
It's the great ambivalence, the uncaring love.
The waking up on summer mornings to the sky cleaved by thunder to
winter evenings blinded by frenzied sunlight.
Our rules mean nothing,
our bodies each faulted flesh.

Stretching a canvas

Layman's oysters shell their ivory
under a swiss army knife, rusted shut.

Trumpets yield to midas,
dancing in the rafters.

Below I leave a thumbprint
on the second layer.

Enshrined lines gasping in rotation
with myriad surface worries.

The staples are never symmetrical
similar to surgery in its way.

Jaunty, singing imperfections
alight in the notion of immortality.

Feynman Dilemma

Quantum meadows make no sound.
You could superimpose the rustle of grass
and/or paper. A layer of comfort
to a two-dimensional abstraction
which has been cast over creation;
cast on my mind as well, or more like:
in the shape of it. As I try to visualise those
geometric diagrams as the structure, we survive in.
Minimalist architecture has forever been in fashion,
but I struggle to see its patterns
as I wait for the bus on a Tuesday morning.

Desynchronisation

Codify the process – a supple and writhing:
                              phosphene phenomenon
                    collapsing in the refractions.
                              Architectures unbound by dissonance,
                    disobedience,
                    radiation.
NOW! Quaking foundations, the electricity unfurls – takes on new
shapes and patterns – inlaid by prior observations. (Absorbed) (flipped)
secluded in the grey – rewound in the infra light cycle.

Reincarnation

After 'Shark Heart Submarine' Dorothy Cross.

I wonder if that heart lies rotting
or has it set to new beat
within a hand-cast metal shell?

Unknowing consumption,
consumptive – anaemic
as its transitive state is consumed

by creatures wriggling
beneath the dirt.
Turning it to that finest of forms,

the particles that end all journeys
are ash/dirt/dust.
The end of all aesthetic,

cultural, and physical metamorphosis
lies beneath our feet
or at the bottom of the sea –

being largely frowned upon
until encased
and placed somewhere important.

Bioaccumulate

A little red stains the cuff,
splinterings out the fine-strung lines.
A little criss-cross stain
staying in place as the protein curdles
and spins little molecules out of cotton.

It sits, shifting brown in thin lines
along my thumb and stretching out to my index finger
thin layers of purple and blue
hammocking the two appendages.

Opening a little as I grip the bike handles.
A little more red for the mix,
catching rain and running pink
down my wrist and out to the roadside.

Lost on the tarmac, a little imprint sits and stirs
with the dirt, and cloud chemicals
caught on a stray heel
that stepped aside to let wheels and feet go past.

Holding back
the laws of thermodynamics from that more primordial state.
Oh, how the earth shall rattle.
As all that rubber repeats and I open bit by bit;

spilling out of the encasement and mixing with the scene
mix, splay, and fade out
like the last imprints of pigment-stained lashes.
What Colours we leave behind!

Anna D'Alton

cipher

one then two dates in   i'm in   i laugh i hook on your messages

    i think   this this could be something   flowing to the edge of

something   catch your big jokes   i try my   dry wit   familiar

    all smooth talk   song links   drunk texts   and what about

your side glance   foot brushing my rib   when you say

    you think something's   missing here   a bit   missing

    don't you think   i think   i can't find missing

i puzzle you   comb signs of curve declining   when you didn't

    want a nightcap   words   stalled out

when you pulled away from   my kiss   at the zebra crossing

    i should have known then   i knew then

Barocco Leccese

When did the dodo become extinct? You ask me over glasses of red wine after our trip to Lecce. Those churches outdo anything we've seen before, façades dripped in gargoyles, cherubs, suns. On the Basilica di Santa Croce, a dodo peered out from between the sheep.

1690, we inform ourselves, on the island of Mauritius in the Indian Ocean. The timeline syncs: a colonial discovery picked out of limestone as news, baroque-style. Then followed an ordinary obliteration, a flightless bird hunted, easy prey for humans and the animals

they brought with them. Observe the stone dodo, learn its lesson and rein in your casually consumptive ways. It's possible to do a thing to death, you know. But of course we don't. It's not an aberration, an irregular pearl, but a violence we keep repeating. *Lonely Planet*

says it's a must-see in this Puglia town, asks us to spare a thought for the Jewish families expelled from the land so the basilica – its dodo, cherub, sheep, disciples – could sit here instead of anywhere else. Nearby a relief of sun and moon look on, flat-faced, implacable.

from Blunt Knife

I

It's laziness to let knives go dull. A lack of pride in my possessions, an absent self-respect. My apathy appears in spots of rust on steel, in the broken tip of one blade and another snapped in three places, a smooth edge serrated to lodge shrapnel in chunks of butternut squash that could have cut my throat.

I inspect the failings of my cutlery drawer: crumbs and mismatched forks, an absent whetstone, a succession of neglected knives. Nothing glints. Not even when I turn the light on, not even when I lean and look at it sideways.

II

She holds a hard-back book in her palm and extends her smallest finger along the spine as leverage. It is a small finger, alert, straining to balance the book so it doesn't topple. She hasn't consciously moved it there, though she feels a pressure on the finger's tendons. It can't keep this up forever. She reads and with the other hand she picks dry roasted peanuts from a bowl. The nuts crunch between her teeth, the paper as she turns the page.

III

An avocado not quite ripe, when sliced in half, resists splitting. Pulled separate, its stone clings in one of the halves, tied to the flesh. I insert my thumbnail, press hard to draw a deep bruise pain and the stone comes loose.

IV

On a quiet day in the office I lift three of the teaspoons I've been eyeing from the container beside the sink. I slip them into my pocket, then into my bag and walk out of the building, no thrill to speak of, only the almost imperceptible weight of the spoons.

V

A soft mood can split on the edge of a knife. I look at myself the wrong way in the mirror, I wait until I'm ravenous to think about cooking dinner, I stub my toe on the threshold and spill my cup of tea down the front of my shirt. I sharpen, harden against everything around me.

VI

The cat has an abscess on his tongue where he licked the sharp edge of a tuna tin that we should not have put in front of him. I see that now.

VII

I can't recall what I was slicing but a Swedish tour leader was following me around the restaurant, making demands. I was filling in for someone else's shift and a group of forty Swedes sat waiting for their scrambled eggs and bacon. I hurried to fetch what they needed, ragged, confused, and underestimated the bite of the knife's fine teeth. Blood dripped through the napkin I wrapped around my left hand, I hurried around, phased, looking for pitchers to fill with orange juice, anything of use. The tour leader followed, asking why I hadn't been more prepared.

Amy Evans Bauer

fer mata

            s unset

let's   start le   t here,
light   en
burd   ened day

                        un civil twilight

c locked face to face to
face past five past six
degrees twi by twi lit

                        civil to nautical twilight

salut e

@ Cat caught in & in
somnia come on in

we are   naut
           with out

b eke
  c all
b eke

nautical twilight

g lad tidings m othered,
      left to right light
un gathers sky

nautical twilight

d arker and d arker
in visible: see shelf
rendered legible at 18°

murderous tilt
of the eye, sea sea TV

LET THEM eat the kitchen SINK
as sea bed's workers
work their night un touchable

astronomical twilight

Lost at Scene
in whylight

let's get lust
    find out
        y our my inside

    b lured lines
        on wet sheets

s ink fur ther
as contours fuzz

                            astronomical twilight

lock ed in in
in decline-able language
    un   safe
as teles cope, *das Fernrohr*

g lass mich in ruhe
      in Holy Babel
to self de scribe

                            nicht nacht

s till dance

she rites
a social s pace

a g rounder
  g lobe

                            astronomical twilight

sonic at lass t
         she w *ave* s
th under   c lap s

for selves in the
sea bound by

sc ored lines
n ever at rest

                            astronomical twilight

knows knots
what she does

she says kno
she said no

she said *nichts*
knots nothings

in to
night—

night *f* all

Note: *Fermata*—in music, a sign indicating a pause of unspecified length; also known as a hold or, when placed on a note or rest, a *grand pause*; known colloquially as a *birdseye* or *cyclops eye*; from Italian *fermare*, to stay or stop. When placed over a bar in a concerto, a *fermata* indicates the point at which the soloist is to play a cadenza—a virtuoso solo passage inserted into a movement, typically near the end. These poems were written at Caroline Bergvall's *NIGHT & REFUGE live writing*, 20 May 2020.

how to hug a piano

racked isn't hard
to master in repeating

rooms—dare thumb
to reach from

least grown finger,
blossom octaved

palm: fathom
outstretched arms

again and again,
lean towards

costly reunion
across sea,

clutch wide wood,
cast keys to shade

with human breasted
bulk; a nipple

to sharpened F,
and gently place

cheek to lid to listen for
friendship of hammer,

resin, felt—
heavy raft through

unchildish past
attuned to many

a—strike it!—
lost disaster

Contact

I do not know
how eggcup clung
to plate's cold
face as it span
rotations through
stunned air.

I cannot feel
the child's confusion
while she does not
duck and hair
greets missile
that spins over

head. I have not loved
the man who set food
in angry flight,
though something
like love creeps
among memories.

Sofa, sink, sister
and vertical space
compose momentary
family portrait. I know
what was on my left and
right. I see what I said

launched the dish—clash
of porcelain with wall
hailed silence. Bread
soldiers who could not
break too hard a yolk lay
guiltily about, witnesses of
who knows what. We

were beyond our
mother (sure of that)
as we visited our blood
in a shock of minutes.
Grown, I gather
what shell knows
peace by peace.

Tom Phillips

Study for a reconstruction

> *working*
> *to distinguish an event*
> *from an opinion*
> —*Roy Fisher, 'The Memorial Fountain'*

A great curve of steel beam –
he's hauling it down the street –
is all grinding, clanging, scraping,
a dissonant resignation.

His is not the only chord.
Rough thumps shake earth
beneath a dizzy clarinet
and a song on the radio
I've not heard for years,
if I've heard it at all.

Coca-Cola fizzes like rain.
Intemperate June washes
the paving stones' lap,
in tune with hesitations.

It's not clear what to expect.
Crowds gather surreptitiously
as if fearing they're unthinkable
at such a time in such a place,
as if improvising harmonies
across all possible keys.

In a café-bar's conservatory
a waiter introduces his accent
like a doctor explaining a symptom
when he thinks it's safe to do so.

We move on
through resurgent rain
and the soft earth scores
our indefinite footsteps
as we climb the sticky slope
to a factory reinvented.

It's where a writer will speak
of anti-monumentality.
I'm with him there –
though in the cool damp outside
fountains assert their part
in the hierarchy where we flounder.

On Shishman, a guitarist
raises his hand and says
the singer in the bar
is worth the interruption.

We have to move on.
On the turning into Chumerna,
a small toad squats in the gutter,
then shrugs, grunts, hops
into a convenient puddle.

Morning will break eventually
and in a quiet entirety
before first tram brakes grind
and the day begins to build
like the *glissando* at the end
of Chopin's *Ballade*.

from English Fortnight

1. Clevedon bus stop

Cross-hairs of wooden beams
on a mock-Tudor terrace can't help
but look like X marks the spot
or a vote cast without hope
in an environment deemed to be hostile.

Greenery wreathes Strawberry Hill,
its cottage gardens' pleasant land
where we're to feel at home –
though swifts distantly remind
we're remote from it still

and questioning bus route information,
acceptable payment methods,
simply lighting a cigarette
has us down as visiting migrants.

2. Portishead revisited

Stories we're at the edge of resurface.
Our once-occupied selves look out
from snapshots that fleetingly recall
a meeting, a marriage, a meal –
although none of those are clear
in stifling pub conservatory air.

Unintroduced, I stumble on names
as if all our lives have been tangential
until we'd been brought together here
for your mother's delayed memorial –

until we'd no choice but to have our turn,
our turn at being the ones who've to manage
familial relations from now on
when surely, surely, we're too young.

Entr'acte 21-22

For this special interim…
        —*W.H. Auden, 'Thank You, Fog'*

The old year has started to dissolve.
Dates ascend their cyclical scale
as cloudbanks descend
and fog and woodsmoke rise.

Ranks of red-barked pines
wait in the mist to be counted –
another calendar emerging
as if dreaming a new sun.

What turns will turn again –
now softening into comfort,
now sharpening into light.

Let this evening bring us ease
before the rigour we'll need afresh
to look into the woods and see.

Lucy Hamilton

Train set. Book. Vinyl. Body.

I

It was a child's garden. The gift was profound. Pleasure flushed hot on my face. My mother signifying me on my birthday. Endorsing a place I had no name for. The doctor stepped between the tracks signals bridges spreading across the bedroom floor. The doctor and my mother handled my body and the Verses lay open on the *counterpane*. A word I didn't know. It jostled in my mind with shop and window. It bounced on the blanket with *camel caravan* which I pictured trotting along the Cromer Road hitched to a Sixties model down from the Midlands. Those kids were our annual beach playmates. It was a child's garden.

II

Facing the impact. Nothing had prepared me as I recovered alone on the sofa with the cover's phonogragh and little dog always the same always different. Choosing through the LPs in my brother's draw-string pyjamas. The dog selecting me for the empty kennel in the courtyard I'd painted blue in an empty wish. The music hit me like a *tsunami* I'd never heard of. Like a wall of water Wagner shocked me. That huge wave engulfed me breathless and spinning in a great blind deafening unknowing drum roll of sensation I would never forget. *Tannhäuser Overture*. My body electrified. I jumped up to conduct. Facing the impact

The absorption of birds

I

It was a signal moment. How could I admit that the story wasn't true. My hands wrestled in my stomach. Plow-right or Plow-wrong. My spirits sank at the prospect. The forest fire hadn't happened. It was homework not hometruth. I stood by Sister Martha's desk longing to lie. Yes I wanted to say. My hands clammy. Yes I fought the flames with my brother's old blazer. Saved creatures screaming out from the undergrowth. Rescued fledglings from scrupulous nests. No I answered. Her praise was so unexpected I flushed to my roots. I returned to my desk light as a bird with a hefty reward. It was a signal moment.

II

Like an art of patience at the ready. I copied birds from my *Observer's* dipping into my mother's childhood water-colours on the Formica table. I wanted to claim I'd seen the hoopoe but needed textual facts. Years followed helping kids love verbs into handmade books. What is accuracy. *Hier j'ai sauvé un rossignol de l'incendie.* I ask my oldest sister if they still chorus in the woods by the Humber. She talks about her daughter in the States. The long caesura is an agonising gulf. But what after all is importance. A labour of lethargy on the alert. Today my beloved receives his first vaccine. Like an art of patience at the ready.

Meccano set. Magic set. Chemistry set.

I

Was there such a thing as truth. I limped home smarting with the groceries. Humiliated by the glib deceit of their explanation. That they thought my nature easy pickings. But next day I saw that a boy had to kill and be killed. A Meccano set could not protect him. My father banned me from reading the Paper. I knew he was cancelling the Cuba nightmares. For me and my twin he ordered *The Children's Newspaper*. I asked for a magic set for my tenth birthday. Conjured a repetitive white plastic egg. For my eleventh a chemistry set. I watched copper sulphate turn blue though the presence of water was elusive. Many tests failed. Was there such a thing as truth.

II

Anyone has to breakdown. Is collapse the failure to see or understand. How history repeats. Its religions as traditional as architectures. We always believed we'd live to see a third world war. A war perpetrated by the first world destroys the third. When something comes between you and your beloved the inner person is hidden from the outside like a stranger. The dear forked creature is visible but the precious inscape is faceless. Now the Leaders have cancelled. My eldest sister cannot travel. She says she'd believed that inner spiritual work could act upon the outside world. Is her sickness the fear that it cannot. Anyone has to breakdown.

Steve Brock

Out of season

sometimes things
just fall together

like the cat
leaping through the hole
in the screen door
to join us for beers
on the back veranda
under midsummer rain

Miles' *Doo-Bop*
playing on the speaker
a CD we wore out
in our youth

there's a fog over the sea
and our garden
is lush and green

it's the end of holidays
and we have the house
to ourselves

you put on a dress
purchased in your 20s
from a boutique
around the corner
of a share house
we lived in

the rain stops
we make love

and doze
late into afternoon

beyond our breath
a plane distances itself
from the world

upon reflection
our youth was something
less misspent
and more indulged

Miles blows
and blows
regaining lost time

Luis

I'd see him
in the food court
sitting alone
in the same black leather jacket
unshaven, long hair
always happy for me
to join his table
and talk about Bukowski,
Pedro Juan Gutiérrez,
Cortázar, the classics
in Spanish and English

he introduced me
to the Korean steakhouse
$13 for a New York cut
cooked by a 5-star chef

Luis worked as a Spanish tutor
and on the side he ran
a rare book business
works he'd collected
in a lifetime of travelling

he told me about a first edition
of Lorca's poetry
he'd let go for $60
a fine edition
but we never
closed the deal

a few months went by
without seeing him
in the food court
and then a mutual friend told me
he'd died suddenly
alone in his apartment

the landlady was at a loss
of what to do with the books
he had no family in Australia

not long after
I moved jobs
to an office
on the other side of town
but still got a hankering
for those steaks
and would walk
the extra few blocks
to the food court
and eat on my own

until one day I went there
and the Korean steakhouse had closed

within another couple of years
they bulldozed the whole place

and all that was left
before the rubble
was the 19th century heritage façade
propped up by an array of steal beams

like a door to a time
I could never return

Aidan Semmens

Of which we speak

in this place too the streets are full of traffic
waving flags of mother tongues
cities illuminated like manuscripts
retelling our origin tales of old

our songs of love and suffering traded
for rights of residency and passage
language exported as commodity
syntax and lexicon susceptible

to the vagaries of commerce and stock
exchanged like pork belly futures
for buttons and beads, Europa
abducted by Zeus as a bull

Orpheus lamenting lost melodies
and trade routes, love conflated
with the Nasdaq Composite
the exchange rate of obsidian to salt

mining of the richest archive
restructuring of signs and tokens
gatherings of pain and celebration
anticipation of traditional motifs

of which we have to speak
a valuation of territory and naming
translation of the ceremony
retailed in another tongue

by deportees burned by a foreign sun
in passages of place and time
the train of argument arrived at
neither here nor there

to say who is now the coloniser, who
the colonised, who become subject
or object of transaction or transgression
your word traded against mine

Transmission

what nameless crimes, what acts
of random grief are committed
in the spaces between channels

what borders, borderlands crossed
by shining and despairing eyes
places of no homecoming

mountains, coasts and hinterland
cities where once was wild grazing
deserts where once there were cities

a landscape of significance
the shape of a cruel geography
a place where flesh meets stone

a language of impermanence
stray acts of mistranslation
among shreds of human kindness

old bones and new blood
invisible in the fog of interference
a transmission beamed

between unconscious states
a dance of death and duty
among buildings torn up

and thrown down in streets
and studios of sharp design –
another show you simply mustn't miss

Holy land

unknown rooms abound below ground
traces of pigment preserved on the statuary
Egyptian blue a possible component
of flaked and forgotten flesh tones

in the ossuary soil nestles inside crania
and some retain scraps of dark hair
thigh bones and skulls neatly stacked
rounded joints and empty eyesockets staring

at Tel Burna near the occupied West Bank
fragments of leopard mandible and a lion's paw
evidence ancient cultic practice
symbols of elite power and control

in a maritime climate the shipping news
rises to a brave crescendo then
sinks in submission
to the transmitting wave

exacting the harshest punishments
on these unwilling travellers
culprits of arcane transgression
unwary passengers of escape

let the bombs fall where they will, artefacts
wield all the power of revered gewgaws
while we sink into beatific TV visions
of a Happy Families Land warm as sunlit water

Daragh Breen

from Quattro Stagioni

3 Oranges in Summer

"the sea's honey is measured on dusk's scales"

the rose of the summer waves
in full bloom
and the heaped hives of fishing nets
piled on the grass
garlanded with sea-bleached
orange buoys

fragments of crab shells
and claws
shattered mid-summer ritual masks
and hoof prints leading down to the
crumbling white honeycomb
that frills the tideline

"the Hunter's moon echoes orange through the centuries"

the mushroom skulls of jellyfish
trailing their prayer beads
came to flab out their flesh
on the salted sands of the west coast
where the sun died,
the whole open wound of their being
splayed on these small wet deserts

for centuries
as they made their seasonal procession
passed the witnessing Skelligs
the local fishermen would row out

and pray with them
as they slowly jostled on the waves
day after day, night after night

when they arrived and crowded on to
the beach of our childhood
we had no idea whose sins they were

"summer's gilded barge sits buoyant in the rare Nile of the sky"

driving west to Bantry
in the early hours after
you got that phone call,
godless and unable
to believe the heatwave
temperature of the haloed dawn

the room was already emptied
when we arrived,
every bowl of oranges
in the wards
having chalked
to white overnight,

and the only movement
was of the peacocks
out in the grounds
that the patients
always mistook
for hallucinations

3 Reds in Autumn

"a red seam appeared across the dark, a trail of embers laid along the horizon"

Sunrise, with clouds,
        the languid
Koi-blemished
        waters
in which
        the blacksmith
dips
        the fresh ingots
of fish.

        The blacksmith
launched
        a floating candle
to try and trace
        where his boy
might have
        washed ashore.

Sunset, with clouds,
        the mother of
a thousand Christs
        waits
by the riverside
        to collect
the spoils.

"the fabric of a ghost laid bare"

When we found our fox
in our shed
she had funnelled her red self
between two wooden boxes

with a hindquarter left in this world
and the medical textbook workings
of its innards cleanly displayed
beneath a flurry of Bluebottles
harvesting vigorously
so as to decimate its diagram,
echoed and mirrored
in the Bluebottles'
frantic movement above
as they wove her ghost
into thin air.

"a mottling of red wings that fails to take flight"

The silent bells of fuchsia
string their dead sound
along the hedgerows,
the bees having muted
their pleated spheres.

Every time the tide retreats
from the Warren
its as if it will never return,
exposing jagged rock
and ghost horses
in the silent channel
of its wake.

Everything appears to be
held in utter suspense
before the light changes,
the water rises,
and noise resumes.

Miguel Otero Silva

translated by Chris Holdaway

from The ocean that is oblivion

7.
"Every instant of your life is a step you take towards death."
                    "Chou-King"

In front of these olive groves and vineyards of Giotto-like friars crying
            out level with the hills,
before this composition of Leonardo that captures cypresses in
            mysterious greens,
at the foot of those azures of Fra Angelico condemned to the heavens
            through the centuries of centuries,
it occurs to no one to think of death.

It occurs to no one to think of death
as long as the light of midday spills its dice cup of white grapes over the grass,
the nightingales spin words of Virgil in the June leaves of an elm,
the rose bushes crash their purple joy against the walls of grey,
and a scent of ripe cherries rises from the hollows.

To no one, I say.
It occurs to no one to think of death
when a blonde woman, fluttering dove unfurled on a stone bench,
smiles at us from a distance—that scatters over her beautiful body—,
and calls out "Miguel" to us, four times "Miguel" with the melodious voice
            of a schoolgirl.

Those who measure the drops of their blood like the grains in an hourglass,
and those who cite the sacred books of China without shaking off the roses
            of dust that cover them,
in vain they mutter to me that to live this light, this voice, this landscape is
            to take a step further towards death,
that to savour the sun of this morning is to deduct it from another morning
            of life.

9.

While I recited Manrique's verse:
"our lives are the rivers
that flow into the ocean
that is oblivion",
she lay next to me without looking at me.

She was silent for a moment without looking at me
and then she answered slowly without looking at me:

– There are rivers that do not flow to the ocean
but to other rivers that carry them to the ocean.

10.

Discovery of the stone:
stone is the recovery of forms and volumes
that were buried by the heel of the wind.

Paraphrase of the lily:
the lily is the revenge of weeds and ferns
that extinguished their greens in the river's clay.

Genesis of the rain:
the rain is the retreat of streams and estuaries
that assail the sky through the arcades of the sun.

Spring of a voice:
your voice, young visionary poet,
tracer of epicycles, explorer of globes,
this voice that bursts from your singular essence
is the undercurrent of the calls of dead poets.
It's the lime of the bones of dead poets,
white seed that germinates on your heart.

17.

Who said that dying was a shady forest,
a howling barrage of stark femurs,
a night cleared by the radiance of scythes,
a thirsty dog barking at the stars?

Who said that dying was a ditch of swords,
a plaster wall with neither thickness nor end,
an air devoid of insects and birds,
a sandbank burning beneath strontium skies?

Who said dying was a seraphic light
a dust ascending in spirals of gold,
an echo of "let's go" towards where we come from,
a burning stake put out by the breath of a god?

Dying is the ocean as Manrique wrote,
the ocean and nothing more.

Marco Catalão

translated by Chris Miller

from The Wings of the Albatross

1.

Epaminondas has never felt *the anguish of the blank page*
If anything causes him anguish
It's not having infinite days and nights
To fill with words
As many blank pages as he wants to

Lining up his verses on the left of the page
Immediately induces
A state of expectation and ferment
That leaves him quite incapable
Of assessing any poem at all
Let alone one of his own

That may be why
He is not excessively concerned
(Despite his all too human vanity)
With the senseless glory of small magazines
Or the ambiguous prestige conferred by doctoral theses

Which show no signs of knowing he exists

Let them ignore him let them despise him
This bothers him no more than the whine of a mosquito

All things considered
What matters to him
Is that vacant space
Where he lines up verses up
On the left of the page

And to feel
During the most fruitful hours of the silent morning
Or the hours of insomnia before dawn
That he belongs to the family of the impatient Leopardi
And the Pessoa of whom no one has yet heard.

2.

The impatient Giacomo and the unknown Fernando

Much more vivid than his colleagues at work
More alive than the strangers on the bus

Populate Epaminondas' daily reality
With questions that distract him from the menu in the restaurant
Metaphors that interrupt the typing of memoranda.

His wife even imagines...
But the teenybopper next door
Or his cousin with silicon implants
Present no risk to his moth-eaten marriage

Unlike
Sophia
Emily
And Wisława

5.

Epaminondas is irritated by the ingenuousness
Of those who think it was just a matter of chance
Or because they died too young
That Kafka and Pessoa remained unknown
Pound lived to be 87 and they put him in jail
Giuseppe Tomasi di Lampedusa had his book published
At a mere 62 years of age
(admittedly he was already dead at 60)
And although he was a prince by birth

He received the title of author only after his death
Epaminondas is irritated by those who praise the great authors of the past
But are incapable of naming a single great author in the present
And still more irritated
Because he sees only mediocrity around him
And among his contemporaries can name
Not by any means a Shakespeare or a Dostoyevsky
Not so much as a Mário or a Vinicius
Epaminondas furiously impatiently scours
dozens of volumes in bookshops and second-hand stalls
hundreds of online sites of obscure poets
All he finds is waste imagery
Flaccid versification
Laughable errors of syntax
By whose death could this bloody mess
Be transmuted into poetry?
Epaminondas is still alive
And irritated the way only the living can be

Concha Méndez

translated by Harriet Truscott

Fear Is Yellow

Fear is yellow. And death
is that sky, precarious
and bewildering.
It's that guiding light –
so we shut our eyes
and follow.
We play long games
in the uncertain miles
as we walk towards
that star – that high final
door-lintel as we step into
the empty.

Yes, I know now cold is white,
and fear is yellow.

Silence

Stone silence felt
on my body, on my soul,
and I, uncertain, under
stone's weight.

Stretched out across the night
– shadow tree, branchless –

Seems the hour's asleep.
Seems like she's not I,
the woman here alone.

Not Air

No, not air
into my lungs. Ice
stilling the feeling
in my blood.
And where I step
ground gapes away,
and what I glance at
darkens.

Daybreak: tears break
my eyes apart.
Not even daybreak yet,
my eyes already gape
in disbelief.

Nights I Like to Walk

Nights I like to walk deserted cities.
My own footsteps sound alone in silence.
Feeling myself walk thus among the sleeping
feeling I'm passing through a boundless world.

All is carved into relief: an open window,
light, a pause, shadow, a sigh…
The streets grow longer. Time stretches out.

I have lived centuries, walking the small hours.

Bar

Bar by the port.

Salt voices and tobacco smoke.

Voyages flicker their film reels on the walls.

One white-suited sailor
deals the cards.

Tricksy mermaids
are hunting down the crew.

– Bar by the port –

An alcoholic breeze.

(One white-suited sailor
drops his cards.
He walks back to the ship.)

I Sing Now

Song I sing now so they hear me
down the reign of centuries,
so they know me living – they,
you, those living then.

Song I sing now for those souls
strung in tune with mine.

Ennio Moltedo

translated by Marguerite Feitlowitz

from Las cosas nuevas

9

With each domestic jolt, we're blown beyond the border. We will end our days in the bunker in Berlin. The country tries to reimpose itself, but the rapid production of paper disappears in a torrent. The system, developed elsewhere over centuries, suddenly dawns, painted on the windows, with everyone reciting the verses once written on the blackboard. Blaring and belting and disco. They switched out the flautist for the computer. Untethered astronauts and local Martians jostle each other in the crosswalk, among dogs and traffic lights; suddenly, they don't recognize each other; confused, they observe themselves, searching for a reason to live. Out there, in no man's land, a poem will be read.

12

for Gonzalo Gálvez

Is it possible, Your Excellency, Your Eminence, that I'm being judged by the newspaper vendor on the corner? He knows me well. I've been his client for years and his stand could easily become a center of investigation and a courtroom open to the public and to the breeze that blows freely from the sea. Corner of Errázuriz and Bellavista. Our day-to-day existence requires a meeting place. The temple of power is always contemptible.

Confined to a high cage in the Coliseum, the parrot's job was to crow, stoke the Romans' zeal for combat. Collapsing the centuries, we have an emperor right here in the highest rungs of the Circus Maximus, corner of Avenida Pedro Montt and La Feria (do/do not confuse this with the slave market). The high cage in our stadium is empty, the messenger bird has flown down to the center of the circus where it parrots imperial memories for the kindly smiling empress and the fawning followers of Caesar and Brutus.

69

And who are you to forbid the flowers of evil?
Are you sick? Admit you're a man of this world.

75

for Eduardo Embry

These were inadequate: The Great Wall of China, The Alps, Hadrian's Wall, The Maginot and Siegfried Lines, The Atlantic Wall (Rommel in charge). Of the Berlin Wall all that remains are hammers and memories, more innocent than the stones of the moon.

But right here we too have relics for the world: two streetsworth of impregnable bricks blocking the sea and sands of Playa Portales and, closer in, the Bicameral Temple and the skyscrapers eternally rising between the rubbish and rags of Augusto's Market (MCMLXXX).

91

Vision I: All the bums of 1973 have turned into mummies. Vision II: All the mummies of 1973 have turned into royalty. Vision III: The rest, naturally, have disappeared.

Giedrė Kazlauskaitė

translated by Rimas Uzgiris

*

literary pregnancy
was the reason i gave
for an academic break

women with bulging stomachs
have gathered here in church
for an embryonic mass and
i hold an anatomic atlas in my hands
with half-dead muscles
twitching spasmodically
when you touch them
while inside my backpack
i have malformed babies in formaldehyde
and a dictionary
of developing latin trees

i sit in the church
among the bellies
reading the stained glass
waiting for my bulge
to show

***

i ravished myself
in the armchair under the laurel tree
with pseudo-sacral music playing
ameno dorime
padre

the girl i was kissing in my dream
turned into my mother
and i woke up ashamed
with a diminished libido
my breasts frayed etc.

her breath at night
is the beat of the waves of my sea
and her stuffed little nose makes
the muffled cries of seagulls

the god of milk and meadows
accompanies the ships
of our evening prayers
becoming my father in the morning
wearing a world-saving vest

their self-ravished daughter
fears two things:
night and day

***

I hadn't yet read Lacan
but already knew there is no woman.
Men were the revelation.

I was afraid to sit next to them on trolley buses,
with their aryan gazes, self-confidence,
man-spreading over a seat and a half.

But I remember what Wisława had told me –
she, who had been slated to be a ballerina, while
wanting to be an artist – we spoke strangely,

with a Petersburg accent, which had been marinated into her
by the desiccated choreographers whom I hated:

grey-haired teachers with black ribbons
who came into the cafeteria leaning on canes
to weigh out the cottage cheese so that Wisława
would stop drawing pictures of food
after she vomited out the box of Napoleon cake.
Oh, how horribly she betrayed everything she had talked about!

Just so she could squeeze with one thigh
into that trolley bus seat.

And I remember what another Wisława had said –
writing about Heraclitus's river, where fish quarter fish –
much later, in that same language, almost forgotten,
but rising up from childhood like a myth –
about our continuously vomited existence:
she didn't lie about liking sentimental postcards,
gilded with sparkles, porcelain sculptures
sweet as cottage cheese cake, swans made of crochet.
She always looked for such in stores that sold kitsch.
She weighed them out like portions of food.
And she could buy so many after the Nobel!
But her words were boats which I secretly sent off
filled with all the men of the *Iliad*,
filled with all my unconstellated instincts,
and I walled the sound away.

This is how birds call to each other
by the river in spring.

Las Meninas

It seems like it happened first in a darkened classroom –
slides of paintings: you had to identify them,
and I did. It's like rummaging through your writings:
the feeling of getting a good grade.

That unknown word, similar to our "menas" – art –
with the meaning of fräuleins, or "girls" in portuguese;
but an infante is by no means simply a princess –
more from the word "infants" – infants for whom there was
so much applause that no shame attached to the name.

Everyone likes a retinue, especially those who applaud;
let's not believe that we are left out.

She's so infantile that she believes Marab Mamardashvili –
that death is only in life; there is no other side to it;
that even in the unconscious, whose disentanglement
is our real life, there are no images of gods.

Yet she is religious down to the bone; instead of prayer,
the radio buzzes with the voice of her loved one,
barely discernible over the enervated waves,
the revelation of the author (or the artist).

Instead of confession, she tries to clean her biography
by controlling her mailbox –
she never liked to find the notes of strangers
in her library books.

I would like to keep just a few letters
where people's politically incorrect vanities
do not appear like the marks of sneakers
on the palace parquet.

Meninas, you write diaries that I can read –
a voyeur who can find confirmation in them
that we are similar, just like me in my notebooks
(though let me not remember where they are).

While the baby learns how to walk (she first
learned how to swim), I can only follow
the sometimes monstrous footsteps
of twenty-somethings in their
vulgarly candid social media accounts.

Unfortunately, my life is literature,
and I don't have any less perverted
hobbies than that.

It's an egotistical interest, for sure –
to catalogue characters, as one director
taught: like hanging clothes in a closet,
not knowing if you will use them or not.

You have to understand their motivations,
so that even a transvestite in the closet
can be matched with the right accessories.

Those meaningless Sapphisms that won't save a text:
that unliterary girl, those friends of no interest to anyone,
appear merely as ballast for the power of society;
that annoying family where everyone
is sick with pathological sentimentality –
I think you all live in the Meninas portrait.

Your reality is now on the other side for me;
at twenty-one I didn't have a girlfriend, or even
the thought of one, but I already had a book.

So I'm spitefully curious as to how
you romanticize author-hood, even though it requires
not just loafing around and loneliness,
but the renunciation of the creative act.

A few years lost to alcohol,
a writing disability, and then you wake up,
looking for the tin chamber pot
that has been assigned to you.

All for the sake of the language with whom
(more than a lover) you not only live, but sleep,
constantly polishing your sentences in dreams.

Notes on Contributors

JOSEPHINE BALMER has published two collections with Shearsman, *The Paths of Survival* (2017) which was shortlisted for the London Hellenic Prize and a Poetry Book of the Year in *The Times*, and *Ghost Passage* (2022). Previous titles include *Chasing Catullus* (Bloodaxe), *The Word for Sorrow* (Salt) and *Letting Go* (Agenda Editions). A *Selected Poetry* from Shearsman is in planning.

DARAGH BREEN has three collections from Shearsman, the most recent being *Birds in November*. He lives in Cork, Ireland.

STEVE BROCK is an Australian poet, with four published collections, including *Live at Mr Jake's* (Wakefield Press, 2020) and *Double Glaze* (Five Islands Press, 2013) and am the co-translator from Spanish to English of the anthologies *Desarraigo: 18 Poetas Transfronterizos,* (Nautilus Ediciones, 2021) and *Poetry of the Earth: Mapuche Trilingual Anthology* (Interactive Press, 2014).

CARMEN BUGAN is the author of nine books including poetry, memoir, and criticism. Her most recent collection of poems is *Time Being* (Shearsman, 2022), and her most recent collection of essays is *Poetry and the Language of Oppression: Essays on Politics and Poetics* (OUP, 2021). Her new and selected poems, *Lilies from America* (Shearsman, 2019), was a PBS Special Commendation. Her memoir, *Burying the Typewriter* (Picador, 2012), won the Breadloaf Nonfiction Prize, was shortlisted for the Dayton Literary Peace Prize and the Orwell Prize for Political Writing, and was BBC Radio 4 Book of the Week. Bugan's work has been translated into Italian, Swedish, Polish, Chinese, and Romanian and is widely anthologised. She is an Assistant Professor of Literature and Creative Writing at New York University in Abu Dhabi.

MARCO CATALÃO (b. 1974) is a leading Brazilian poet and playwright. The poems here are drawn from *As asas do albatroz* (The Wings of the Albatross) which won the Rio Prize for best Brazilian book of poetry in 2018. This is a book-length comical study of a mediocre but devoted poet, Epaminondas, working out his destiny in a land where there are too many poets and too few readers. Its title refers to Baudelaire's poem 'L'Albatros'.

ANNA D'ALTON is from Mullingar and lives in London. Her poems have appeared in journals in Ireland, the US and elsewhere, most recently *Porridge* and *Superpresent*. She is working on her first pamphlet.

CARRIE ETTER's most recent collection is *Grief's Alphabet* (Seren, 2024).

AMY EVANS BAUER is lives in London. Her five-chapbook sequence includes *and umbels* (Jonathan Williams Chapbooks prize, 2020) and three Shearsman titles. Her chapbook *Suffrajitsu* came out with Earthbound Press this year. Her poetry features in *Chicago Review, Queenzenglish.mp3* (Roof books, 2020) and elsewhere. She is co-editor of *The Unruly Garden: Robert Duncan and Eric Mottram, Essays and Letters* (Peter Lang, 2007). She has written criticism for the British Library's Sound and Vision blog, and BBC Radio 4.

MARGUERITE FEITLOWITZ is the author of *A Lexicon of Terror: Argentina and the Legacies of Torture*, and the translator of volumes of plays by Griselda Gambaro and Liliane Atlan, as well as *Pillar of Salt: An Autobiography with Nineteen Erotic Sonnets* by Salvador Novo. Her chapter on the Chilean director Marcela Said was included in a special issue on *Latin American Women Filmmakers of PostScript* (vol. 40, Nos 2 & 3, 2021).

MISCHA FOSTER-POOLE's work has previously appeared in magazines including *Poetry Wales, Perverse, Tentacular, Poetry London, 3:AM, Hotel, Stride,* and *X-Peri*. His first collection was published by Veer in 2018, and he has a collaborative visual poetry collection with Ali Graham forthcoming from Hesterglock Press.

LUCY HAMILTON's third Shearsman collection is *Viewer / Viewed* (2023). Prose poems from her work-in-progress, *Reverse : Inverse*, have appeared in *The Fortnightly Review, Tears in the Fence,* and in *Dreaming Awake*, an anthology of contemporary prose poetry (Madhat Press, 2023). She has worked as editor, writer and organiser for Cam Rivers Publishing and the annual Xu Zhimo Poetry & Arts Festival based at King's College Cambridge, and has held several residences in China. She was awarded the Xu Zhimo Lifelong Achievement Award 2023.

ELLEN HARROLD has recently published poetry in *Shearsman*, as well as *York Literary Review, Causeway/Cabhsair,* and *Skylight 47*. She is currently working on a panel discussion for a conference with Newcastle University on the use of art as a research tool while trying to find time to write more poetry between that and her day job. She lives in Ireland.

CHRIS HOLDAWAY is a poet from New Zealand. His book *Gorse Poems* was published in 2022 by Titus Books, and the quasi-title piece from there ('Gorse') was included in *Shearsman* 123 & 124. He has work in the major NZ journals like *Landfall*, in Australian outlets such as *Cordite*, and numerous US periodicals including most recently the *Western Humanities Review*. He studied translation at the University of Notre Dame.

HUW GWYNN JONES is retired and lives in Orkney. He comes from a line of poets in the Welsh bardic tradition, though he denies ever having worn a druidic robe. His work has appeared in *Acumen, Tears in the Fence, Lighthouse, Stand, Obsessed with Pipework* and *The Galway Review*. His debut pamphlet, *The Art of Counting Stars*, was published in 2021.

GIEDRĖ KAZLAUSKAITĖ (b. 1980) studied Lithuanian literature at Vilnius University, where she tried writing a doctoral dissertation. Her first book, *Bye-Bye School!* (2001) was prose, her second *Hetaera Songs* (2008) was poetry. For this book she was awarded the Young Jotvingian Prize. Giedrė's third book *Postils* (2009), written together with Father Julius Sasnauskas, presents commentary on the gospels. Her fourth book, a poetry collection, *Las Meninas,* came out in 2014 and won the Jurga Ivanauskaitė Prize. In 2016, her third poetry collection, *Singerstraum,* won the Writer's Union Prize and the Most Creative Book of the Year Award. She published her fourth poetry collection, *Amber Room,* in 2019. Since 2010, she has served as editor in chief of the bi-weekly cultural periodical *Šiaurės atėnai*.

Jazmine Linklater is a poet & writer currently based in Manchester. Her pamphlet, *Figure A Motion*, was published in 2020 by Guillemot Press. She previously published two pamphlets of poetry: *Toward Passion According* (Zarf Editions, 2017) and *Découper, Coller* (Dock Road Press, 2018). She currently works for T-Junction International Poetry Festival and Carcanet Press, and sits on the editorial board for Broken Sleep Books.

Concha Méndez (1898–1986) was one of the Generation of '27 in Spain, a friend of Lorca and student of Alberti, and her work is currently enjoying renewed interest in Spain after some years of neglect. She died in exile in Mexico.

Sujatha Menon is a British Asian poet and musician based in the Midlands. Her poems have been published internationally and she is the author of *The Glass Puddle* (Vole, 2021) and *Night Swan to Nigg* (Cromarty Arts Trust, 2022). Her forthcoming full collection titled *Microscopia* will be published this year by Pindrop Press. In addition to writing poetry, she has performed and written songs with the band Satsangi for 20 years. They have collaborated with and supported many artists and musicians, have been broadcast on BBC radio and MTV, featured in magazines such as *Rolling Stone* and have travelled internationally to share their music. More information on Sujatha's work and projects can be found at sujathamenon.com

Chris Miller is a critic and translator who has published translations from *brasileiro* in *PN Review* and *Warwick Review* and in pamphlet form (Clutag Press).

Ennio Moltedo (1931–2012) was described by Raúl Zurita as "one of the finest, greatest, most curious and honourable poets of Chile." He has been compared with Cavafy for his allegiance to a place at once mythic and mundane; with Char, for the inventiveness of his political poems; with Saba for his mastery of extreme concision.

John Muckle lives in London and has worked as a teacher and editor. In the eighties he was founding editor of Paladin Poetry and *The New British Poetry 1968–88* (with Allnutt, D'Aguiar, Edwards and Mottram). His most recent books are *Mirrorball* (poems), *Late Driver* (stories) and *Snow Bees* (a novel), all from Shearsman Books.

Miguel Otero Silva (1908–1985) was a Venezuelan poet, member of the radical Generation of '28, exiled at various points during the Gómez and Jiménez dictatorships. He also founded the newspaper *El Nacional,* which continues today. It was Otero Silva who commissioned for his newspaper the first of what would become Neruda's *Odas Elementales,* and for that contribution to poetry alone he deserves international recognition. His appears to be the first occasion that his work has appeared in English, apart from a part of a poem quoted in Guevara's *Motorcycle Diaries.*

Tom Phillips is a UK-born poet, playwright and translator living in Bulgaria where he teaches at Sofia University. His poetry and translations have been extensively published in the UK and internationally and his own work has been translated into more than a dozen languages. Recent publications include, as editor, *Peter Robinson: A Portrait of his Work* (Shearsman Books, 2021) while Geo Milev: *Poems and Prose-poems* is due to be published by Worple Press in early 2025.

Paula Sankelo lives in Longyearbyen, Svalbard. An environmental researcher by profession, she currently works as an editor in a Finnish culture journal *Elonkehä*, and as a receptionist in Svalbard museum. She has recently published her first poetry collection in Finnish (Warelia Publishing, August 2024). The poems published here are selected from this collection and translated by the author. Her English translations have also been published in *PolarLit: The Svalbard Literary Journal*.

Ian Seed has published seven collections with Shearsman, most recently *Night Window* (2024), as well as a translation, *Bitter Grass* (2020), from the Italian of Gëzim Hajdari. His translation of Max Jacob's *The Dice Cup* was published by Wakefield Press (2022). More information at www.ianseed.co.uk.

Aidan Semmens lives in Orkney, and has several collections to his name, including four from Shearsman. His most recent is *The Jazz Age* (Salt Publishing, 2022). He also edits the online magazine, *Molly Bloom*.

Simon Smith is a poet and translator living in London. He has previously published ten collections of poetry including a selected poems and a complete Catullus translation. His latest books are *Last Morning* (Parlor Press, USA) and *Municipal Love Poems* (Shearsman Books) which appeared as companion volumes in 2022. 2022 also saw the publication of *Source* (Muscaliet Press), a collaboration with artist Felicity Allen and representation of Rimbaud's 'Le Bateau ivre'. He is presently working on a book-length series of prose poems, *The Magic Lantern Slides*.

Between 1991 and 2007 he worked at the Poetry Library in London and taught creative writing and poetry at London South Bank University, The Open University, and the University of Kent from 2006 to 2022. He is Emeritus Reader in Creative Writing at the University of Kent.

Harriet Truscott studied literary translation for an MA in Creative Writing at UEA (2022–23). The first poem included here was Commended in the Stephen Spender Prize for literary translation, 2023. Other translations of her work appeared in a recent edition of *Modern Poetry in Translation*.

Rimas Uzgiris is a Lithuanian/American poet and translator writing in English. Born, raised and educated in the USA with a PhD and MFA, he is the author of the poetry collections *North of Paradise*, and *Tarp* [Between] (poems translated into Lithuanian). He has translated seven poetry collections from Lithuanian, and his work has appeared in *Barrow Street, Hudson Review, The Poetry Review, Poetry Daily* and other journals, and has been nominated for the Pushcart Prize. Recipient of a Fulbright Scholar Grant, a NEA Translation Fellowship, he teaches at Vilnius University.

9 781848 619340